Spitfire

By **DON PATTERSON**

Illustrated by Sonny Schug

Hindsight Limited, PO Box 46406, Eden Prairie, MN 55344.

ISBN   1-929031-18-1
Library of Congress   99-097213
Copyright © 2000 by Hindsight Limited. All rights reserved.
Printed in the U.S.A.
First Hindsight ™ printing, January 2000

PICTURE CREDITS
Many thanks to the following organizations for giving permission to reprint
illustrations and text used in the "In Hindsight" section of this book:
p. 92 Air and Space, Bullfinch Press, New York
(Courtesy of the Smithsonian Institute)
p. 94 Profile Publications, Albatross D5, Surrey, England
(Courtesy of the Imperial War Museum)

Written by Don Patterson
Illustrated by Sonny Schug/Studio West
Edited by Mary Parenteau
Production by Kline/Phoenix Advertising Graphics

*To those with the
wisdom to do what's
right, when it's needed.*

TABLE OF CONTENTS

"SPITFIRE!"

CHAPTER ONE

ONLY AUTHORIZED PERSONNEL

Colonel Harrison, the Commanding Officer of Hampton Airfield, stood at the window in his office peering through a pair of binoculars. Turning back and forth, his square shoulders stretched the seams of his neatly pressed Royal Air Force uniform while he searched the sky.

Finally spotting what he was looking for, Harrison quickly focused his field glasses. Out in the distance, a formation of RAF Hawker Hurricanes was flying just above the horizon. Not having seen action for days, the pilots of the 14th Squadron were sharpening their skills by practicing combat tactics over the countryside surrounding the airfield.

"Captain Dawson really has those lads snapping up there," Harrison said to himself while observing the fighter planes climb and then dive for the tree tops.

After several more minutes of turning and twisting, the squadron leveled out from their maneuvers and approached the airfield to land. One by one, the RAF fighters smartly set down on the grassy airstrip, ending their training mission. When the last Hurricane touched earth, a proud smile stretched across Colonel Harrison's face.

Even though the practice flight had ended, Harrison continued to observe the activity on the field. While watching the line of fighter planes taxi to the hardstand, he noticed a group of people gathered by one of the maintenance hangers. The cluster of men and women were bent over, picking something up from the ground.

Colonel Harrison shouted for his secretary, Susan Winslow, "Susan! Come in here!"

"Colonel, what's wrong?" she asked while pulling at her jacket to straighten it.

"Who is that down on the field?" Harrison demanded, pointing at the men and women outside. "And tell me what they're doing!"

Susan stepped to the window. Scanning the field, she saw the people carefully picking up spent bullet casings and other bits of metal.

"They're picking up
scraps of metal for recycling,
sir," she replied.

"Who authorized them
to be on the base?" Colonel
Harrison sternly asked.

"No one, really," Susan explained. "They
just come here once a month and pick up the scrap
metal lying about. It's for a good cause, sir."

Colonel Harrison crossed his arms in a huff,
"Those people are not authorized to be here!
Look, Susan, I'm getting real heat from Fighter
Command about unauthorized personnel on the
base. I just received another memo about it today."

"But sir," Susan interrupted, "They help us
by returning the metal scraps to be reused for
building new fighter planes."

Unimpressed, Harrison replied, "What if
one of those people got hurt? What if a pilot, like
that Gainey character, pulled some idiotic stunt
such as a low level fly-by and crashed his plane
down there?"

Susan rolled her eyes at the Colonel's out-
landish suggestion. "But Colonel, even Lieutenant
Gainey knows that low level flying is expressly

forbidden by RAF rules."

"That's exactly my point Susan," Harrison firmly replied. "Everyone knows that RAF rules also forbid unauthorized personnel! Now there'll be no more discussion. Go down there and send those people home!"

"Yes sir," Susan complied in a resigned voice as she turned to step out of the office.

"Susan", Colonel Harrison called out, "there's...well...one other thing." Struggling to find the words, he continued, "I'm afraid that means your brother Harry, too."

Twelve year old Harry Winslow lived with

his mother and sister, Susan, on the Winslow farm bordering Hampton Airfield. Living so close to the RAF fighter base, it had become an important part of their lives. When the war started, Mr. Winslow left to serve in the British Intelligence. Susan returned home from college to help her mother. In order to earn some extra money she took a job on base as Colonel Harrison's secretary. It also allowed her to keep an eye on her brother, Harry. A frequent visitor to the base, Harry loved the pilots and planes of Hampton Airfield. They filled an emptiness in his heart while his father was away in London.

Susan stopped in her tracks upon hearing the harsh order and pleaded, "But Colonel, being around the pilots is so important to Harry. Sending him away will break his heart. Isn't there anything else we can do?"

"I'm not happy about it either," Harrison barked. "I know how close he is to Dawson and the others, but the lad could get hurt around here. You must tell him to stay away."

Harrison snatched the letter from Fighter Command regarding unauthorized visitors and held it up to Susan, "These are my orders. Tell

Harry that six years from now he can enlist and earn his RAF wings. Then I'll make it my duty to keep him on the base twenty-four hours a day. But until then, rules are rules!"

Susan was ready to beg Colonel Harrison to reconsider. But when she looked at him, she could see the strain in his face. The Colonel was clearly upset with the letter from Fighter Command. Nevertheless, she knew no amount of begging would stop him from carrying out his orders.

Colonel Harrison was a career RAF man. He joined the service in 1918, during World War I. A natural combat pilot, young Alfred Harrison scored four victories over enemy fighters in just three days. At the time, it was an RAF record. But before he would battle the enemy again, the Armistice was declared and the war was over. Young Pilot Officer Harrison never had a chance to down a fifth enemy plane and achieve the fame of being a fighter ace.

After the war, Harrison chose to stay with the RAF. Even though the status and acclaim of being an ace eluded him, he was highly regarded for his leadership. Alfred Harrison was known as a man who could get things done. In 1939, when war threatened again, he was assigned command of the RAF fighter base at Hampton.

Now, as base commander, Colonel Harrison was responsible for the operation of Hampton Airfield according to RAF regulations. Harrison enjoyed having Harry around as much as anyone, but he had to obey orders. RAF rules were made for everyone's safety.

With a nod of her head, Susan reluctantly acknowledged the Colonel's command to dismiss all the unauthorized visitors, including Harry. Although sending the people picking up scrap metal away seemed harsh, telling her brother he wasn't allowed on the base would be heart wrenching.

Regardless, Susan always obeyed the Colonel's orders to the letter. Marching out of the Operations Building, she walked to the field and in a determined voice sent the group of unauthorized scrap collectors home. Then she went looking for Harry.

While searching for her younger brother,

Susan half-hoped she wouldn't find him. If Harry
wasn't with the men out on the airfield she would
be spared the heartache of sending him away.
Harry worshipped the pilots and crews of
Hampton. In return, they had made him a part of
their RAF family. The rule on unauthorized personnel was clear, but Susan wondered who would
suffer the most, Harry or everyone else at
Hampton Airfield.

CHAPTER TWO

THE NEW ARRIVALS

Finished with their training flight, Dawson and the other pilots taxied their Hurricanes to the hardstand in front of the maintenance hangers. As each pilot cut power, the thunderous roar from the engines died down. When the whirling propellers stopped, the awaiting air crews quickly surrounded the planes in order to refuel them and meet with the pilots. After every flight, the pilot and his flight mechanic would discuss any repairs or changes needed to keep the airplane in peak fighting condition.

Throwing back the glass canopy to his cockpit, Captain Dawson called out to his mechanic, Sergeant Thomas Pendleton, "Thomas, you really tightened up that rudder for me."

Releasing the straps to his seat, Dawson climbed from the cockpit and stepped onto the wing of the plane. The stocky Sergeant stretched out his hand to help Dawson hop down to the ground.

"Was it too tight, sir?" Pendleton asked.

Dawson straightened up from his jump to the dirt and replied, "Not at all! She kicks from side to side, with no slip. It's just the way I like it."

Proud of his work, Pendleton replied, "I aim to please, sir!" He finished by punctuating his words with a sharp salute.

Captain Dawson smiled at his mechanic's playful show of respect and then looked down the row of fighter planes on the hardstand. Turning to walk away, Dawson said, "Well, Thomas, I'd better see to the others. Carry on!"

"Have a good evening, sir," Sergeant Pendleton responded in a preoccupied tone. Constantly fretting over Dawson's Hurricane, he was already reaching into the engine housing to check the oil and coolant levels.

Glancing over his shoulder, Dawson noticed how quickly Pendleton went to work on the plane. "You know, Thomas," he called back to the diligent flight mechanic, "it's only because you do your job so well, that I get a chance to do mine."

"Just remember me at Christmas, sir!" Pendleton replied laughingly. With his head deep inside the engine housing, the Sergeant's voice

Dawson said, "Well, Thomas, I'd better see to the others..."

echoed out across the field. Then, in a quiet whisper he spoke to himself, "With you in the air, we're all a little safer."

Captain Dawson walked down the hardstand calling to his pilots, "On to the briefing room, gentlemen! Follow me."

The other pilots hurried to finish the conversations with their flight mechanics. Catching up to Dawson at the door to the Operations Building, the close knit group of fliers walked down the hall and filed into the briefing room.

The Squadron Leader, Captain Dawson, made his way to an oak desk at the front of the room, while the rest of the men took their seats. Dawson had been in the RAF for four years. In addition to being an outstanding combat pilot, he had earned leadership of the squadron by being a wise decision maker in times of crisis.

Confidently stepping behind the desk, he began erasing some old notes scribbled on the blackboard in order to draw example pictures for discussion. After wiping the board clean, he took a piece of chalk and started sketching airplanes in different positions. The other pilots watched while Dawson outlined the steps used in the maneuvers they performed during their training flight.

Looking over his illustration, Dawson explained, "I've drawn our positions for the bank and roll. Now we can talk about what we did right, and what we did wrong out there today."

Dawson turned from the blackboard to face his men. Clapping his hands to clean them of chalk dust, he began, "Okay lads, let's start with..."

The Squadron Leader stopped in mid sentence. Dawson expected to see a group of attentive pilots in front of him ready to discuss the training flight. Instead, they were all crowded around the window like schoolboys watching the first snowfall.

Bewildered at the men's behavior, Dawson asked, "What in blazes is so interesting out there?"

With wide eyes, Lieutenant Hyatt looked back at Dawson and shouted, "Captain, they're delivering the 'Spits'!"

Interested, Dawson stepped past the desk to join the men. Scratching his head, he mumbled to himself, "I thought the new Spitfires weren't going to be delivered until next month."

Working through the crowd of pilots straining to see the new airplanes, Dawson peered out the window. Through the filmy glass, he saw a group of trucks pulling three Supermarine Spitfire fighter planes to the blast pen shelters at the far end of the

field. Even though gray canvas still covered most of the cockpit on each plane, the wide wings and sleek body hinted at the gracefulness of the new fighters. With his pilots so distracted by the arrival of the Spitfires, Dawson knew continuing the meeting would be a waste of time.

"Attention!" Captain Dawson barked.

Hearing the snap in his voice, the men immediately turned to face their Squadron Leader. In a more casual tone, Dawson finished, "All in all, we had a good training run today. You're dismissed."

Captain Dawson stepped to the side and held the door open for the other pilots. Flashing quick salutes, they bolted out of the room and rushed to the airfield to examine the new Spitfires.

CHAPTER THREE

"SPITFIRE!"

Captain Dawson slowly walked across the field, trying to hide his excitement about the Spitfires. Racing to the line of earthen blast pens housing the planes, the younger pilots swarmed on the fresh fighters. Only Captain Simms, second in command of the squadron, patiently waited for Dawson to join him.

"Ted," Simms called to Dawson, "who would have thought they would be here a full month early?"

Fascinated by the three new planes, Dawson replied, "They're surely a sight to see, aren't they, Andy?"

Together, the two Captains stepped to the first Spitfire in the row. The veteran pilots examined the sculpted lines and smooth silhouette of the powerful fighter plane. Then a distracted Simms jabbed at Dawson with his elbow to get his attention.

"Look," Simms said in a low voice, "even the 'old man' is coming over to see them."

Dawson turned to see Colonel Harrison approaching. Without question, the three Spitfires had become the center of attention throughout the entire airfield.

Colonel Harrison had been requesting the new fighters for quite some time. The Spitfire was faster and more maneuverable than the rugged Hawker Hurricane. Harrison knew his men stood a better chance against the enemy if they were flying Spitfires.

"There they are, gentlemen," Colonel Harrison announced to Simms and Dawson, while pointing at the new planes. "Spitfires will eventually replace all the Hurricanes in our squadron. They've already switched over in some of the other fighter groups."

The three men stood together silently, gazing at the sleek fighters. Then Harrison stepped over to the cockpit of one of the planes and ran his hand across the side of the fuselage.

"With 1500 horsepower, six guns, and a top speed of 385 miles per hour, our pilots should gain a real advantage over the German Messerschmitts we've been fighting."

"Colonel, when will they be air ready?" Captain Dawson asked.

"Actually, Ted, the only thing holding us up right now is that we can't get a Spitfire flight instructor out here for another week. Supermarine is making the planes faster than they can teach us how to fly them."

Captain Simms nervously cleared his throat and asked shyly, "Who is going to get first crack at learning how to fly these birds, Colonel?"

"I'll decide that a week from now, when the instructor gets here," Harrison replied. "Until then, gentlemen, make sure your rather curious pilots don't scratch the paint on my new airplanes!"

With that, Colonel Harrison marched back to his office in the Operations Building. Both Dawson and Simms grew red faced at the Colonel's remark. All they could do was watch while the young pilots under their command crawled upon the new fighters like children on a playground.

Sheepishly leaning over to speak in Dawson's

ear, Simms asked in a whisper, "Should we bother telling them what the Colonel said?"

"What's the use, Andy?" Dawson replied while shaking his head. "They're so excited they won't listen to us anyway. You and I might just as well plan on coming back here tonight to polish over any scuffs the men leave when they're done."

As the sun set on Hampton, the three new airplanes were still the center of attention. The only pilots who weren't talking about the Spitfires over dinner in the mess hall, were the ones still out on the airfield examining the planes where they stood. "Spitfire" was the last word on the lips of practically every man in the squadron before retiring to bed. The potential life saving power of the new fighters made each RAF pilot sleep that much better.

CHAPTER FOUR

AN UNAUTHORIZED VISITOR

A new day arrived all too soon to Hampton Airfield. Before the sun climbed over the tree tops, the hardstand was busy with ground crews preparing the squadron's Hurricanes for flight. Over the last several weeks, the number of German air raids on English targets had decreased. In fact, it had been several days since the 14th Squadron last "scrambled" into action. Even though no mission was scheduled for the pilots, an enemy attack could happen at any moment. In preparation, the squadron's planes were required to be ready for combat at all times.

After checking the progress of his men maintaining the Hawker Hurricanes, Sergeant Pendleton walked down the field to examine the Spitfires. Shying away from the commotion caused by their arrival yesterday, Pendleton was happy to have a quiet moment by himself with the new planes.

Rubbing his hand along the tip of the wide

wing, Sergeant Pendleton whispered to himself, "You are a beauty, aren't you?"

"She sure is!" a small voice called back.

Startled, the gruff Sergeant spun around searching for who made the reply. Then he spotted young Harry Winslow. Harry's tousled brown hair was barely visible above the long stretch of hedgerow fence that separated Hampton Airfield from the Winslow farm. A frequent visitor to  the base, Harry was practically an adopted member of the RAF family.

"They really are something to look at, aren't they, Sergeant?" Harry excitedly shouted from behind the bushes.

"Stop sneaking up on me like that, Harry!" Pendleton playfully scolded his young friend. "You wouldn't want me to mistake you for an enemy spy and lock you up in the stockade!"

Smiling at the good-natured teasing from Sergeant Pendleton, Harry stretched up on his toes to keep his head above the hedgerow fence. Earlier, Harry's sister Susan had informed him of Colonel

Harrison's orders regarding unauthorized visitors. Harry felt very disappointed, but he accepted being banished from the base. At least he could watch the activity on the airfield from the Winslow side of the fence.

"Sergeant Pendleton," Harry replied, "you wouldn't throw me in prison. But I guess Colonel Harrison would!"

Recognizing the point of Harry's comment, Sergeant Pendleton tried to explain.

"Now Harry," he started in a sympathetic tone, "you're being too hard on the Colonel. Everyone knows about the unauthorized visitor rule. You have to understand that the Colonel is stuck. He's the commander, so that makes him the one who has to enforce the rules. I've served under a lot of RAF officers and I'm telling you, Colonel Harrison is the best. But Fighter Command has given him orders. When head-quarters gives an order, you obey. If you don't, you'd better have a good reason."

A frustrated Harry complained to his friend, "I know. Sis told me all about the rules. And mom told me I have to stay on my side of the fence. But it doesn't seem fair. I've always tried to help around here. I thought Colonel Harrison liked me."

Sergeant Pendleton wanted to comfort the young boy. Stepping over to the fence, he noticed how Harry was struggling to keep his head above the top of the hedge. Pushing the bushes aside to make a gap, he reached for Harry's arm and pulled him onto the airfield side.

Then he told the boy, "You're one of us, Harry. We all count on you. Colonel Harrison does too, but..." The Sergeant was at a loss for words.

Glad to be standing on the airfield again close to his friend, Harry thought about everything Pendleton had said. He knew it wasn't really about fairness. He also knew that Colonel Harrison and his other RAF friends had to follow regulations.

Harry anxiously dug the toe of his boot into the grass. Then he asked abruptly, "Sergeant, are they going to fly the Spitfires today?"

"No, probably not today, lad," Pendleton replied, relieved to talk about something else. "Colonel Harrison's orders are to wait until the Spitfire flight instructor arrives in a week or so."

Surprised the pilots would need someone to teach them how to fly, Harry put his hands on his hips and said, "I can't believe Captain Dawson is going to wait for a silly flight instructor."

"It's the Colonel's orders, lad," Pendleton explained. "The pilots can't fly 'em, so I'm supposed to hold off arming or fueling them until I receive my instructions."

Harry was disappointed the graceful Spitfires wouldn't be flying anytime soon. Then he asked, "Don't you know where to put the fuel or how to load the machine guns?"

"Of course I do, Harry," Pendleton shot back. "I've been preparing fighter planes for years. They're all pretty much the same."

"Well," Harry replied, "don't you think Captain Dawson knows how to fly? Wouldn't it be just like him to march out here later today and take off in one of these Spitfires?"

Sergeant Pendleton looked hard at Harry. The twelve year old was right. It would be just like Captain Dawson to clear things with the Colonel so he and a couple others could fly the new planes at the end of the day. And if they weren't ready, Dawson would come looking for his trusty flight mechanic to get them ready. On top of that, the proud Sergeant felt a little insulted at the thought of a civilian teaching him how to prepare and maintain an RAF fighter plane.

But more importantly, the veteran crew chief knew the mechanic's unwritten rule that having unprepared fighter planes sitting on a military airfield could be dangerous. In an emergency, Dawson or one of the other pilots might need to scramble one of those planes. If it wasn't ready for combat, someone could get killed.

"Considering everything," Sergeant Pendleton said, "maybe I should get these planes prepared, just in case. I'll supervise a crew to fuel and arm all three Spits so the pilots can take

them up at any time. I think the Colonel would agree that having the planes ready and waiting would be best. But still, let's not broadcast what we're doing. You know, don't 'let the cat out of the bag'. Right, laddy?"

"Yes sir, Sergeant. You can count on me to follow your orders!"

Harry's response was interrupted by Colonel Harrison calling to Sergeant Pendleton from the steps of the Operations Building.

"Sergeant Pendleton!" Harrison shouted. "We need to update our flight preparation checklist for the Spitfires."

"Yes sir! I'll be right there," Pendleton called back.

Trying to shield Harry from the Colonel and Fighter Command's unauthorized visitor rules, the stocky sergeant quickly lifted the boy over the bushes. Instantly, Harry was back on the Winslow side of the fence.

"Go now, run along," Pendleton said, as he winked at Harry. "The Colonel has been under a lot of pressure about those rules lately. If he sees you, there'll be the Dickens to pay!"

"Hey, I'm on my side of the fence," Harry

replied defiantly. Sergeant Pendleton tilted his head and gave Harry a stern look. Realizing his RAF friend was just watching out for him, Harry continued with some apology in his voice, "But I'll get out of here so there's no trouble for anyone."

Ducking down behind the hedge, Harry ran off toward the maintenance hangers. As Harry slipped out of sight, Sergeant Pendleton called out, "Remember, lad, don't let the cat out of the bag!"

CHAPTER FIVE

SCRAMBLE THE HURRICANES

The morning sun continued to creep higher in the sky while the men on base waited for the "scramble" alarm. Although most of the pilots passed the time gathered out on the field, Dawson and Simms used the idle moments to help keep their squadron ready. Today, they were sorting through shelves of spare parts in the maintenance hangers. After a thorough inventory, Dawson put together a list of needed supplies.

"Andy, I want you to drive to Chester and get these replacement engine parts before we run out," Dawson told Simms and handed him the list. "I can just imagine trying to explain to the Colonel that we can't fly because we ran out of piston rods and manifold gaskets."

Simms nodded his head, "That would be an ugly conversation. I'll take Hyatt and Gainey and make quick work of it."

The two pilots were startled when behind them, an excited voice asked, "Can I go with you?"

Trying to avoid Colonel Harrison, Harry was now skulking about the hedge where it ran behind the maintenance hangers. Although most twelve year old boys would find other ways to spend their time, Harry Winslow was happiest when he was with his RAF pilot friends.

"Blast it, Harry!" Dawson chided in a teasing tone. "You'll do me in before an Me 109 does! Quit sneaking around like that."

"Sorry, sir," Harry apologized while standing on the tips of his toes in order to keep his head above the fence. "I'll try harder not to surprise you next time. But sir, please can I go with Captain Simms?"

Dawson looked into Harry's begging brown eyes and half-heartedly tried to scold the endearing young boy. "Harry, the word is out. According to Colonel Harrison, you're not even supposed to be here."

Then Dawson looked at his friend and fellow pilot, Captain Simms, and he continued, "But then again, it's been so quiet lately, I don't see any

harm in it, just this once. It's up to you, Andy. Do you have room in the lorry?"

Simms looked at the eager Winslow boy and in a fatherly tone replied, "We'll make room. In fact, I consider it my duty. After all, a ride into Chester would keep the lad off the base now, wouldn't it?"

Dawson laughed at the clever application of the unauthorized personnel rules. Then he turned back to Harry and nodded his acceptance to the boy's request.

"Thank you, sir!" Harry excitedly called to Captain Simms. "I'll get on the..."

"Wait right there, lad," Dawson interrupted. "It's okay with Andy and me, but you still need to clear this with your sister first."

"Yes, sir! I'll go get her permission," Harry shouted as he quickly climbed through the bushes onto the airfield. Eager to find his sister, Susan, he rushed off to the Operations Building.

While watching Harry scamper away, Captain Dawson turned to Simms.

"Promise to take care of that lad, Andy. Make sure nothing happens to him. He's the most important thing we've got around here."

Knowing full well what Dawson meant, Captain Simms agreed. "I'll promise you that. No harm will come with three RAF pilots looking out for him."

Harry ran up the steps to the Operations Building. Then he bolted into the offices where his sister worked, startling Susan at her desk.

"Harry!" Susan warned. "If Colonel Harrison sees you, there's nothing I will be able to do to help."

"It's okay, Sis," Harry quickly explained. "I just need your permission to go to Chester with Captain Simms. If you let me go, you won't need to worry. I'll be off the base."

Susan couldn't argue with Harry's logic, but was a little uneasy about letting him travel so far from home. However, when a young corporal, sympathetic to Harry's situation, announced that Colonel Harrison was crossing the field on his return to the Operations Building, Susan quickly agreed.

"You mind Captain Simms," Susan told

Harry, "and go straight home when you get back."

While Harry was asking Susan for permission to go to Chester, Simms, Gainey and Hyatt loaded into a truck. Lieutenant Hyatt drove the canvas covered transport up to the steps of the Operations Building and stopped to pick up Harry.

Dawson watched the spry Winslow boy jump down the steps and hop into the back. When they drove off through the front gate, he felt relieved to see them finally on their way to get the necessary supplies.

Shortly after the truck left, a clerk spotted Dawson in front of the hanger and called out to him. "Captain Dawson," the corporal shouted, "Colonel Harrison wants to see you immediately."

Captain Dawson hurried to the Operations Building, and walked down the hall to Colonel Harrison's office. After a quick knock on Harrison's office door, Dawson entered.

"Colonel, you wanted to see me?"

"Yes, Ted," Harrison replied. "Controllers at RAF headquarters have picked up a German formation to the south, headed for Dover. I want you to scramble the squadron to intercept. How many pilots do you have active right now?"

"Nine," Dawson replied. "I just sent Simms, Gainey and Hyatt to Chester for parts and supplies."

Harrison nodded and thought out loud, "Headquarters is also scrambling the 62nd Squadron...still, take your nine Hurricanes and help those lads out down there."

"Yes sir!" Dawson said with a salute, and rushed to the airfield.

For the first time in days the scramble alarm sounded. The remaining pilots of the 14th Squadron dashed to their planes. Dawson met his men on the hardstand and briefly informed them of their mission to Dover.

Seconds later, the thundering roar of fighter plane engines echoed across the countryside. The powerful Hawker Hurricanes raced down the airfield and jumped to the sky. Within moments of being airborne, the squadron had formed up on Captain Dawson's lead. Then the nine rugged fighters gracefully banked to the southeast and passed out of sight.

CHAPTER SIX

INTERCEPT AT DOVER

Captain Dawson keyed his radio, "Men, we're off to help the lads in the 62nd Squadron beat back a formation flying for Dover. Stay on my heading and we should

intercept just past the coast. It's my guess that the 62nd will get there a bit before us, so keep your eyes open for the fight."

The skilled pilots acknowledged Dawson's command. Then the radio fell silent while the airmen prepared for combat. Barely ten minutes out from Hampton Field, the nine Hawker Hurricanes roared across the northern end of the city of Dover. Dawson and his squadron contin-ued east over the English Channel, in search of the enemy bomber formation.

Once more Dawson keyed his radio, "What's our motto, lads?"

Eight voices boomed in Dawson's headset, "Send them packing before they reach land!"

"Roger! I'm glad you all remember," Dawson replied to his fellow pilots.

Ahead of the RAF planes, clouds dotted the sky making it difficult for the British pilots to spot any other aircraft. Dawson squinted as he tried to see an outline or any movement that would expose the incoming enemy planes.

Then, from the corner of his eye, Dawson thought he saw something. Focusing his attention to the left of their formation, Dawson strained to see anything other than the swirling patches of white and blue. Blurred spots seemed to move along with the clouds.

A moment later, the radio crackled with the low voice of Lieutenant Collin Mathews. "Mathews here, Captain. There's quite a row up ahead, at three o'clock low."

Dawson leaned forward in his cockpit and looked to his right in order to see what the lieutenant had spotted. Mathews was right. In front, and a bit below right of the RAF formation, the sky was filled with airplanes in the throws of battle.

Just as Dawson had predicted, the 62nd

Squadron had intercepted the incoming German formation first. With the targets now in sight, Dawson dismissed the blurred spots he noticed earlier.

"It must have been the reflection of our planes in my canopy," he thought.

The nine Hurricanes of the 14th Squadron rapidly closed in on the dogfight in the sky. Dawson counted twenty He 111 bombers, and with them, a fighter escort of a dozen German Messerschmitt 109s.

"Let's mix it up lads!" Dawson barked into his radio. "Break on my mark!"

Continuing his approach to the battle, Captain Dawson adjusted his goggles and shouted, "Break!"

Throwing the yoke forward and right, Dawson rolled into a dive. The rest of the pilots followed their Squadron Leader. In a split second, the 14th Squadron joined the pilots of the 62nd in their defense of Dover. The addition of nine more RAF fighters instantly created even more havoc with the incoming German formation.

However, the cunning Me 109 fighter escort sent to protect the German bombers refused to retreat. Regardless of being heavily outnumbered, the deadly Messerschmitts continued to swarm on the British planes. The raging battle filled the sky with crippling gun fire, trails of vapor, and danger!

CHAPTER SEVEN

HAMPTON FIELD IS
UNDER ATTACK

Back in Hampton County, a green and brown camouflaged transport truck rumbled down the road toward the air base. Captain Simms, Lieutenant Gainey, Lieutenant Hyatt, and Harry Winslow were returning from Chester with a load of spare parts and supplies for the squadron.

Hyatt swerved the truck along the rough roadway attempting to avoid the ruts and potholes. Bouncing in the passenger seat, Captain Simms struggled to complete the volume of paper work that was generated by each supply requisition.

"Now I know why Ted sent me for this stuff instead of going himself," mumbled Simms.

"What was that, Captain?" asked a nervous Lieutenant Hyatt.

"Nothing, Hyatt!" Simms snapped. "Just keep driving!"

Hyatt gripped the steering wheel a little tighter. Already a bit anxious about driving with

Simms, Hyatt couldn't help but wonder what he did to upset the Captain. Forever in search of mischief, Lieutenant Gainey took great pleasure in making matters worse by criticizing Hyatt's driving.

"Hyatt, if you keep driving like that, we'll hit a tree for sure!" Gainey teased. "Thank goodness there's only a mile left to base. I think I might be safer in a dogfight with two Me 109s than riding with you!"

Young Harry Winslow had spent enough time around the pilots to know when it was best to say nothing and just enjoy the playfulness of the men. This was one of those times.

Simms looked up from his paperwork and barked at Gainey, "That's enough, Lieutenant!" Then he turned to Hyatt, "Just get us home in one piece, Hyatt. That's all I ask."

Returning his concentration to the clipboard, Captain Simms signed his name one last time. With a theatrical stroke of the pen, he finally completed the volume of forms. Stretching his arms in front of him, Simms then began to chide the two young RAF pilots.

"A trip with you two lads is like..."

But Simms' scolding was cut short by a thundering explosion from just ahead. Startled and confused, the three men looked at each other. Then a second explosion ripped through the countryside.

"The airfield!" shouted Gainey. "That came from the airfield. Come on Hyatt, hurry up and get us back to the base!"

"He's right, Hyatt. Let's move!" Simms ordered.

Hyatt stepped hard on the gas pedal. In response, the truck lurched forward, rushing the passengers the last long mile back to Hampton Airfield. The loud blasts they heard were joined by more earth shaking explosions as they passed through the front gate. Screeching to a halt in front of the Operations Building, the three pilots and Harry jumped from the truck and surveyed the chaotic scene.

The base was under attack! German Me 109 fighter planes and deadly Junkers Ju 87 dive bombers, called Stukas by the British airmen, were descending on the base with a rain of machine gun fire and bombs.

Surprised by the German attack, the RAF ground crews scurried to their appointed battle stations. Most of them took positions manning anti-aircraft guns surrounding the airfield. Within moments, the British guns were spitting rounds into the sky, trying to ward off the ferocious German planes.

"Simms!" Colonel Harrison shouted from the steps of the Operations Building, "I need you, Gainey and Hyatt in the air! Now!"

Simms called back to the Colonel, "Where's the rest of the squadron?"

"They were scrambled to Dover just over an hour ago," Harrison informed the startled Captain. "If you don't get in the air soon, they won't have much to come back to. Now make for your planes, and we'll provide cover while you take off!"

Then Colonel Harrison noticed Harry beside the truck. "Simms," a strict but concerned Harrison shouted, "send the Winslow boy home! He'll be safer at his house. Get him away from the field. Now!"

Simms saluted to acknowledge his Colonel's

commands. The deafening roar from the
punishing enemy planes drowned out any further
attempt to speak.

CHAPTER EIGHT

THE HURRICANES ARE LOST

Following Colonel Harrison's orders, Simms turned and grabbed Gainey and Hyatt by their arms. Directing them toward the airfield, he shouted, "Go on, men! We need to scramble our planes! Now!"

Captain Simms knelt down to speak to Harry, "Run home, Harry! Run as fast as you can! Hurry!"

Frightened, Harry nodded to Simms. Then he bolted across the field, racing toward the hedgerow fence and the safety of home.

In front of the maintenance hangers, the three remaining Hawker Hurricanes were waiting for their pilots. Members of the ground crew feverishly finished loading the machine guns with as many rounds of ammunition as possible.

Another group of men started the fuel-thirsty engines. Simms watched the propellers spin faster and faster, signaling that the rugged fighters were ready. Rushing across the field toward their planes, the three pilots were handed their flight vests and headgear by Hyatt's flight mechanic. Quickly adjusting their equipment on the way, the brave fliers were undaunted by the scream of diving enemy aircraft, crack of gunfire, and thunder of explosions that enveloped the airfield.

Less than fifty yards from the awaiting planes, Simms stopped the two younger pilots.

"Okay lads," he explained in a winded voice, "the south end of the field looks in the best shape. Now, once you're off the ground, climb like mad. We'll need altitude if we're going to out flank the German fighters." Simms looked into the eyes of other two pilots and demanded, "Got it?"

Gainey nodded his head while he finished tightening the straps of his flight vest.

Hyatt snapped the chin strap on his head gear and replied with a simple, "Roger, old chap!"

"All right, the planes are ready!" shouted Simms.

Captain Simms surveyed the airstrip one last time, but was horrified when he saw the slender frame of young Harry out in the middle of the field suddenly caught between attacking enemy planes and exploding bombs.

"Oh heavens above!" Simms yelled, "Hold up men, I have to get Harry!" Dropping his parachute to the grass, he tore down the field calling back, "I have a promise to keep."

Simms ran as fast as he could to save the petrified Winslow boy. Looking up, he saw a German Me 109 diving on the field toward Harry. Racing across the battered turf, Simms was still too far away to help. The veteran pilot could only watch the scene unfold.

Aware of the threatening German plane sweeping down on him, Harry fell to his knees, defenseless. But while Harry crouched helplessly on the grass, the diving Me 109 pulled up, without firing a shot. A moment later, Simms reached Harry and fell on top of the twelve year old sprawled on the field.

Huddling over Harry, Simms shouted in an anxious voice, "Harry, are you all right?"

The terrified boy

collected himself and nodded his head, yes.

"Perhaps now you understand why Colonel Harrison can't risk having unauthorized visitors on the base."

Struggling to put on a brave face, Harry was unable to hold back his tears. "I might be unauthorized, but they're unwelcome!" he cried pointing up at the German planes. Still shaken from the incident, Harry embraced Simms and shouted, "That German pilot could have killed me!"

Simms held the boy as tight as he could and said, "Yes, Harry, he certainly could have fired, but he didn't."

Captain Simms scooped Harry up into his arms, and started to run back to where Gainey and Hyatt were standing. On the way, Simms continued, "Remember, Harry, enemy or not, German pilots have honor, just as we do. It's not our job to shoot at twelve year old boys."

Meanwhile, the German Stukas persisted to rain terror down onto the airfield. The menacing gull winged attack planes were the picture of German air power. When the Stukas dived to drop their bombs, sirens fastened to the wings screamed to the ground below for the sole purpose of terrifying their victims. Even the hardened veterans were frightened by the pitch of the siren and the knowledge that a deadly bomb would soon follow.

The end of Simms' message to Harry was drowned out by the roar of another thunderous explosion. Dangerously close to the point of impact, the other two pilots waiting for Simms were knocked to the ground by the furious concussion.

Shaken, Gainey and Hyatt climbed back to their feet. Regaining their senses, the combat pilots couldn't believe their eyes when they looked at their planes. In front of them, the three Hawker Hurricanes, ready for flight just an instant before, were now nothing more than hulks of burning, twisted metal, spewing thick black smoke into the air.

Simms finally reached the other two stunned pilots. Trying to catch his breath, he set Harry down and stared at the smoldering planes.

"Blast those devils! The Hurricanes are lost!" he screamed.

Gainey looked at Captain Simms and shook his head, "It's a good thing you ran for Harry, or we would have been in those planes when they

"Blast those devils! The Hurricanes are lost!" Simms screamed.

were hit!"

"He's right, Captain," agreed Hyatt. "We can all thank Harry for that. But what should we do now?"

"We might as well get behind one of our anti-aircraft guns and try to shoot some of the buggers down," Gainey suggested in a resigned voice.

The men scanned the field looking for cover while the German planes regrouped to continue their attack on the base. Anger and frustration flamed inside them, but the three RAF pilots seemed frozen. All they could do was watch their planes continue to burn out of control.

Frightened and dazed, Harry struggled to remember something he knew was important, especially now. Sergeant Pendleton had given him an order earlier. Something about keeping a cat in a bag. Then Harry realized the important point wasn't about cats or bags, it was about the Spitfires!

Through the din of explosions a familiar small voice pierced the air. "The Spitfires!" Harry shouted. "You still have the Spitfires!"

CHAPTER NINE

FIRE UP THE SPITFIRES

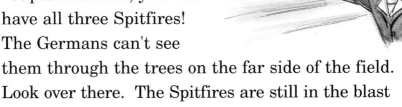

Harry continued shouting over the rumbling explosions and gunfire, "Captain Simms, you still have all three Spitfires! The Germans can't see them through the trees on the far side of the field. Look over there. The Spitfires are still in the blast pens, just waiting for you!"

Harry's message ringing in their heads, all three pilots turned in the direction of the three new Spitfires.

"He's right, Andy!" Lieutenant Gainey yelled over the fighting. "The lad's right. We can fire up the Spits!"

"The Spitfires aren't ready!" barked Simms. "By the time we get them prepared, the Germans will be long gone and the field will be ruined."

Gainey and Hyatt hung their heads. They were fighter pilots without planes.

Harry looked at the frustrated men. He knew the Spitfires were ready, but telling the pilots would be disobeying Sergeant Pendleton's orders. Observing the chaos on the airfield Harry realized that regardless of what was said earlier, Sergeant Pendleton wouldn't want the airfield destroyed. Harry decided it was best to let the cat out of the bag. Saving Hampton was definitely a good reason.

"But they are ready!" Harry shouted to Captain Simms. "Sergeant Pendleton was going to get them prepared before we left for Chester! If Sergeant Pendleton said he was going to ready those planes, you can bet they're ready."

Simms was amazed. "I don't know how you know these things, lad," he said, "but I'm glad you're one of us!" Then he turned to Gainey. "Go get Pendleton and turn over the engines to the Spitfires. We're taking them up!"

Like a bullet, Gainey ran off toward the maintenance hanger to find Sergeant Pendleton and collect a crew to start the brand new Spitfires. Simms and Hyatt watched him shout and point to a group of men helping with an anti-aircraft gun by the last hanger. The makeshift crew quickly organized. Gainey signaled back to Simms with a thumbs up gesture.

Amid the sod and shrapnel hurling through the air, Colonel Harrison ran across the field to reach Captain Simms and the others.

"Andy," Harrison called out, "it's no use. Let's get to the shelter!"

"Colonel," Simms replied, "we're going to scramble the Spitfires."

Harrison snapped at the idea. "They're not ready, and you haven't had any Spitfire flight training. You'll get killed just trying to take off!"

While Simms and Hyatt argued with Colonel Harrison, Lieutenant Gainey, Sergeant Pendleton, and the crew drove to the Spitfires at the far end of the airfield. Pendleton directed the men through the shortest preflight preparation necessary to put the Spitfires into the air. In less than a minute, the planes were ready, confirmed when the engine of each Spitfire turned over on Thomas Pendleton's command.

Puffs of white smoke spewed from the exhausts of the Spitfires. The spinning propellers chopped at the air. Sergeant Pendleton had brought life to the once quiet combat fighter planes.

"Colonel, look!" Simms pointed at the idling Spitfires. "It's just stick and rudder. You were one of the best. Of all people, you should know that's all there is to flying any plane."

Harrison was amazed to see the Spitfires prepared for flight, but still disagreed with Simms' plan to fly them. Regardless of the ready condition of the planes, Harrison knew Simms played down the danger of piloting untried aircraft. The safety of his men was always the Colonel's top priority.

Simms continued, "Colonel, if we don't take them up, those Stukas will destroy them where they stand, as well as everything else on the base!"

The ground shook as Simms' message was reinforced by a series of explosions from the German dive bombers.

After a brief pause, Colonel Harrison shouted over the roar of more gunfire, "Go on men, take the fight to them! Your chances up there or down here are the same. At least up there, you can help us all."

Then Harrison grabbed Harry Winslow and

ran for shelter. Simms and Hyatt scrambled to the waiting Spitfires.

Already strapped into the cockpit of one of the planes, Lieutenant Gainey watched the other two pilots make their way across the field. When Simms and Hyatt reached the idling Spitfires, Gainey called out, "This one is mine. You two can toss a coin for yours!"

Hyatt jumped into the plane next to Gainey, and Simms mounted the last Spitfire.

"I hope you can drive this better than that lorry!" Gainey yelled to Hyatt.

Hyatt looked at Simms and then turned back to Gainey, "Stick and rudder, Brian! That's all it is, just stick and rudder."

Gainey nodded his head at Hyatt's brave comment, and closed his canopy. Hyatt and Simms followed suit, shutting the canopies to their Spitfires in preparation for take off.

Strapped in his seat, Simms plugged in his radio and called to the other two pilots, "Are you with me lads?"

Simms was relieved

Gainey and Hyatt followed their Captain...into the smoke filled sky.

to know the radio worked when his headset crackled with both Gainey's and Hyatt's response.

"Yes, sir!" they chimed in unison.

"All right," Simms continued, "we get one chance at take off, then remember to climb as quickly as possible. When the Germans see us, they'll come with a vengeance, I'm afraid. Just stay with me and climb."

Captain Simms pushed the throttle forward and his Spitfire responded with remarkable power. Hyatt and Gainey followed Simms' lead. The three new RAF fighters lurched from the safety of the hidden blast pens and raced down the airfield at a breakneck pace.

All three pilots were anxious to get airborne in order to avoid the craters and holes that now scarred the runway. Pulling back on the yoke, Simms felt his Spitfire readily pitch up. Gainey and Hyatt followed their Captain on his rapid climb into the smoke filled sky.

CHAPTER TEN

SPITFIRES DEFEND HAMPTON

As soon as the three Spitfires were airborne, Captain Simms radioed the other two pilots, "Get a feel for the controls now, while we're climbing. When we reach six thousand feet, we're going to roll and dive to engage the Messerschmitts."

Simms noticed Hyatt and Gainey working the flight surfaces of their Spitfires while they gained altitude. A veteran pilot, Captain Simms was surprised at how well his new airplane responded to his control.

"Captain," Gainey radioed to Simms," this thing handles like a dream!"

"Bloody well does, Captain," Hyatt confirmed.

"Well, gentlemen, I'm glad you feel you're experienced Spitfire pilots after simply climbing to six thousand feet," Simms sarcastically called back to the other two young pilots. "But now the time has come to dive in and prove our worth. Break on my mark!"

Simms threw the control stick over and rolled

his Spitfire into a dive. Gainey and Hyatt followed. As they dove for the German Me 109 fighters, Simms had a clear view of the airfield below, and suddenly realized just how much damage had been done.

Smoke was rising from the hardstand area at the north end of the field, mostly from the three destroyed Hurricanes. One hanger had collapsed to the ground and was burning, threatening to start the other hangers on fire as well. At the south end of the field, several fuel trucks and field equipment had also been hit by the enemy Stuka dive bombers. Worst of all, the landing strip itself had been reduced to a treacherous stretch of craters and rubble.

The three powerful Spitfires immediately closed on a group of four Me 109 fighters firing on the airfield. Surprised by the RAF fighters, the squad of German planes instinctively split up. Rolling left to follow one of the Me 109s, Simms was pleased with the sheer power of his Spitfire, especially when he lined up right behind his target. Simms quickly maneuvered, trying to place his opponent in the crosshairs of his gun sight.

"She is a little lighter on the touch than my

Hurricane," Simms thought to himself. "But stick and rudder just the same."

Skillfully stalking the German fighter directly in front of him, Simms murmured under his breath, "Come on...come on. Got em!"

Simms let loose a burst of machine gun fire that smashed through the tail and fuselage of the Me 109. When the German plane turned to clear the rain of bullets, Simms fired more rounds into the wings and engine of the enemy fighter. The damaged Messerschmitt lurched, trailing smoke, and then slid along an uncontrolled path to the ground below.

Chasing the second Me 109, Lieutenant Hyatt tested his new plane. The German pilot dove for the tree tops and Hyatt rolled his Spitfire in pursuit, just as in the training flight with Captain Dawson the day before. For a brief instant, Hyatt's gun sight filled with the black cross painted on the side of the German fighter. Triggering the red button on his control stick at the precise moment, the guns in Hyatt's plane trained on the enemy in front of him.

In a desperate move, the pilot of the Me 109 tried to climb out of danger, but to no avail. Hyatt's guns had damaged the plane's engine, leaving it choking for fuel and powerless. As Hyatt raced by, he watched the crippled Messerschmitt stall in the air and fall back into the tree tops at the south end of the airfield.

Meanwhile, the other two Me 109s had turned to pursue Lieutenant Gainey. A natural pilot, Gainey found himself using every ounce of power in his 1500 horsepower Merlin engine, as well as every piloting trick he knew, to outrun the enemy fighters. Streams of tracer bullets ripped past his cockpit while he rolled and twisted in a desperate attempt to shake the Germans.

"Lets try climbing," Gainey thought to himself, and pulled back on the control stick of his plane.

Instantly, Gainey was pushed back in his seat as the Spitfire pitched up in a steep climb. But the two Me 109s closely followed Gainey's move.

"All right," he thought, "let's try a dive."

Gainey threw the yoke forward. Pitching down, the Spitfire hurtled earthward. Still, bright tracer bullets continued to fire past the canopy of his plane. Leveling out and rolling right, Gainey began to turn.

"How tight can you turn?" The young Lieutenant shouted out loud.

The Spitfire's wings tipped sharply as Gainy held the stick hard right. While he continued his turn, the German Me 109 fighters that had followed him so closely, began to spread out in the sky.

Gainey found his answer! The Spit could circle tighter than the German fighters. Within moments, his tight turn allowed him to reposition on the tail of one of the Me 109s. Trying to concentrate, Gainey shook his head to stop the spinning sensation he felt from his hard turn. With a couple of strained blinks of his eyes and a deep breath, the young English pilot focused on his gun sight, preparing to fire upon the fighter that had threatened him earlier. Now it was the Me 109's turn to bank and roll, twist and climb in order to avoid Gainey's gunfire.

CHAPTER ELEVEN

REPAIR THE DAMAGED AIRFIELD!

Together, Colonel Harrison and Harry Winslow watched the battle overhead from one of the anti-aircraft gun bunkers. The Stuka dive bombers had dropped their brutal payload of bombs and cleared the area, except for five that had been shot down by the RAF ground crew gunners. However, still continuing to attack from above were eight Me 109 fighters against the three Spitfires.

Watching his pilots work to outmaneuver the German Messerschmitts, Harrison shouted, "Give it them back, lads! Show them the kind of pilots you really are!"

While the outnumbered Spitfires valiantly battled above, Colonel Harrison's attention turned to the damaged airfield. Soon Dawson's squadron of fuel starved Hawker Hurricanes would be returning. Harrison knew they would need a place to land, and worried about the dangerous condition of the airstrip.

"Pendleton," Colonel Harrison called to the busy sergeant feverishly feeding shells to the anti-aircraft gun. "While our lads keep the Germans busy up there, I want you to mark out a smooth runway so Dawson and the rest of the squadron can land!"

"Yes sir, Colonel!" Sergeant Pendleton replied and jumped out from behind the barking field gun.

Pendleton raced to the maintenance hanger area to gather the additional men and equipment necessary to mark a safe landing strip. Surveying the damaged airfield, Pendleton shouted to the other men, "The west end of the field is the least damaged. We need 300 yards of smooth turf for the Hurricanes and Spits to land."

The makeshift repair crews darted through smoke and jumped over bomb craters in order to make their way to the west end of the field. While most of the men began filling holes and removing debris, Pendleton placed large orange markers on the turf. The orange markers traced a safe landing lane the returning pilots would be able to see from the air.

"Go get more men to help fill these holes!" Pendleton ordered to one of the crew. "If a wheel catches in a crater like that, it will pitch the plane's nose into the dirt."

More and more men from around the base ran out to the field to help repair the landing strip. Up above, the three Spitfires struggled to protect them by engaging the menacing Me 109 fighters at every turn.

Simms radioed the other two pilots, "Keep between the men on the ground and the enemy fighters, at all costs!"

Each time an enemy plane would attempt a run on the field, somehow, at least two of the protecting Spitfire's countered with a hail of gunfire. Although Simms and his men were successful at warding off the German fighters one at a time, when the Me 109s regrouped above, it became clear that the Germans were changing their tactics.

CHAPTER TWELVE

THE 14th SQUADRON RETURNS

"They're going to run on the field all at once!" Hyatt warned Simms over the radio.

Even though the RAF pilots had whittled the German squadron down, when Captain Simms looked up through his canopy, he could see the last six German planes regroup for another run on the airfield. Below, Simms watched the brave crewmen feverishly repairing the field while depending on the Spitfires to keep them out of danger.

"We can't stop all six at the same time," Hyatt continued.

In a determined voice Simms called to the other two pilots, "Do the best you can gentlemen. Let's at least shake them up!"

At Simms' command, the three Spitfire pilots hurled themselves head on at the flight of attacking Me 109s. On the ground, Harry and Colonel Harrison watched the battle turn. The enemy planes raced to attack the men working on the landing strip. At first, Colonel Harrison quietly cheered as he watched Simms, Hyatt and Gainey close on the diving Me 109s.

"Come on, Simms. Yes, yes, head them off! Get as many as you can. We'll take care of ourselves down here."

Then realizing there was no way the three RAF planes could hold off all six enemy fighters, Harrison shouted to warn his men on the airfield, "Take cover, everyone. Take cover!"

Dropping their shovels and diving to the ground, the men on the field covered their heads to protect themselves as best they could. Colonel Harrison grabbed Harry and held him tight, prepared to sacrifice himself in order to shield the boy from harm. Harry, wrapped in the Colonel's arms, buried his head into the chest of the strong RAF commander.

While the men below fell to the ground, roaring gunfire from the British Spitfires collided with two of the German fighters, stopping them well short of the cratered field. But an instant later, the distance between the Spitfires and the remaining attacking planes evaporated. Four of the menacing Me 109s screamed past the oncoming

RAF planes, and continued their deadly run at the men on the field below.

The Spitfires banked hard to correct their path in order to pursue the remaining Messerschmitts. But, it was too late. Even the powerful Spitfires couldn't turn fast enough to catch up to the German fighters racing past them.

Sadly, the English pilots were too far away to be of any help to the men on the ground. As the four remaining Me 109s closed on the field, the helpless men below braced for the deadly crack of machine gun fire. The ear splitting roar of airplane engines intensified as the planes came closer and closer.

Oddly enough, the thunder of engines roaring across the field seemed to be coming from behind the men as much as in front of them. Frightened, but even more confused, the men on the ground rolled over to see what was happening. When they peered into the sky, their eyes widened at the miraculous sight. Barely ten feet above them, the circular RAF insignia on the bottom of the wings of the 14th Squadron's rugged Hawker Hurricanes passed in a flash.

Captain Dawson and his exhausted Hurricane

pilots screamed over the pock-marked airfield. Realizing the life threatening situation, Dawson led the returning RAF squadron on a dangerous low level fly-by, racing to intercept the deadly German Messerschmitts before they could reach the men on the field.

Like an arm sweeping dishes off a table, the line of sturdy RAF fighters swept across Hampton Field. Firing head on into the group of enemy planes, Dawson and his men forced the Germans to break off their attack. In a panic, the last four Me 109s scattered an instant before they reached their target.

Amazed, the men on the ground climbed to their feet and watched the battle between the RAF and German planes. Thankful to be alive, the men cheered at the sight of the nine Hurricanes sending the last of the enemy threat running for home. In one well-timed pass over the airfield, Dawson and his pilots saved Hampton from disaster.

After driving off the German fighters, the Hurricanes circled the airfield. Wary of any remaining enemy aircraft, they searched the skies above Hampton and surveyed the damage below.

Dawson and his pilots save Hampton from disaster.

Concerned with landing on the crater-filled runway, Dawson ordered his fuel-starved squadron to stay in the air as long as possible. Silently, he watched the ground crews feverishly work to repair the field before the exhausted planes dropped from the sky.

"Form up on me," Dawson ordered into his radio, "including you, Spitfires!"

The entire 14th Squadron regrouped, all of the pilots taking their usual positions in formation. When Captain Dawson looked to his right, he saw Captain Simms waving at him from the new Spitfire.

Simms keyed his radio, "I guess now we know who gets to fly one first, eh Ted?"

Dawson retorted, "If I knew the Spitfires were ready, I would have taken it easy!"

"So you were pushing hard to get back," laughed Simms. "Were you worried about us?"

"Worried?" Captain Dawson asked. "What harm could come with three RAF pilots watching over the place? It was just that our fuel gauges were getting low, old man!"

"Well, we're all glad you made it back in time," Simms replied.

Captain Dawson nodded his head and laughed,

"It's nice to know you can still appreciate the Hurricanes!"

Then he called to the rest of his pilots, "Listen up, gentlemen. The lads on the ground have marked the field for landing. Stay in the lane, and be prepared for some rough spots."

On the ground, the anxious air crews watched the pilots skillfully land their aircraft on the narrow makeshift runway. The mix of Hurricanes and Spitfires made their way to the end of the field. With smoke still billowing up from the destroyed Hurricanes and the maintenance hangers behind them, the pilots lined their planes up 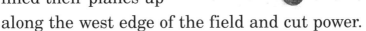 along the west edge of the field and cut power.

Captain Simms threw back the canopy of his plane and jumped to the ground. Ducking under the wing, he walked over to meet Hyatt and Gainey. The three pilots instantly began to blurt out stories of their experience in the new Spitfires. Simms teased Gainey and Hyatt about learning to fly a Spitfire the "hard way." More importantly, he understood just how lucky they were to have lived to tell about it.

Further up the row of airplanes, Dawson stepped down from his Hurricane and was immediately greeted by Sergeant Pendleton.

"Your timing was perfect, Captain!" Pendleton exclaimed. "You saved the day! And with Captain Simms and Lieutenants Gainey and Hyatt up in the Spits, those Germans didn't have a chance!"

Dawson replied, "Our intercept at Dover took longer than expected. Funny thing, on the way I noticed something in the clouds. But once we joined the 62nd Squadron fighting the German formation, it never occurred to me another group was on the way to attack Hampton. After the fight there, we were running out of fuel and needed to land. When we got back to the airfield, we had no choice but to clear the way."

Then Dawson added with a wry grin, "I'm glad you and the others were able to hold out as long as you did. It's sure lucky those Spitfires came from the factory fueled, armed, and ready to fly. Isn't it, Thomas?"

Growing red-faced, Sergeant Pendleton

avoided the Captain's
question and began to poke
at the numerous bullet
holes that pierced Dawson's
Hurricane. As usual, Pendleton complained about
the condition of the battle damaged fighter plane.

"Once again, I must say with all due
respect, Captain, I am tired of fixing all the holes
that end up in my airplane every time you use it."

"Thomas," Dawson chided back with a
smile, "hopefully you'll fix those holes better than
the ones you fixed on the airfield today!"

CHAPTER THIRTEEN

A NEW MEMBER

Five days had passed since the attack on Hampton Field. Although the RAF fighter base was fully operational again, Colonel Harrison was swamped with the paperwork involved to requisition repairs and replacement supplies. Working his way through the pile of tedious forms, Harrison welcomed the distraction of a knock at his door.

Susan Winslow poked her head into the office and announced, "Colonel, Captains Dawson and Simms, Sergeant Pendleton and Mr. Harry Winslow reporting as ordered."

"Thank you, Susan. Send them in," Harrison replied.

Captain Dawson quickly stepped through the door. Right behind him, followed Simms and Pendleton. The RAF members snapped to attention in front of Colonel Harrison's desk. Finally, a timid Harry Winslow cautiously stepped into the room. He sheepishly assumed a position close beside Dawson. Standing in the doorway, just out

of sight, Susan nervously watched.

Harrison studied a report and after a long moment looked up from the pages.

"Captain Dawson," the Colonel asked in a rigid tone, "are you aware that you violated RAF rules regarding dangerous low level flight when you returned to the airfield five days ago?"

"Well...yes sir, I did," Dawson replied with a little hesitation in his voice. "But it was the only way we could intercept the Me 109s running on the field and protect the men."

Colonel Harrison eyed Dawson, seemingly unimpressed with his reason for violating regulations. Harrison shifted in his seat to focus his glare on Sergeant Pendleton.

"Sergeant Pendleton," Harrison barked, "are you aware that you violated a direct order by prematurely readying those Spitfires for combat?"

Pendleton swallowed hard and replied, "Yes sir, but combat aircraft should be ready at all times. It could save a pilot's life."

Again, Colonel Harrison seemed quite uninterested in any explanation. Then the Colonel stood up from his chair.

Scowling at Captain Simms he asked, "Captain Simms, do you make it a habit to argue with your commanding officer regarding standing orders about piloting untested aircraft?"

Simms began to stutter, searching for the right words to say. "No sir, I don't...well at least, not if..." Simms collected himself and finished, "We had to do something to save the base."

Colonel Harrison shifted and looked out the window for a long moment, his hands clasped behind his back. He remained deep in thought. The only sound heard was the ticking from the clock on the wall.

Finally turning to face the group who were

nervously standing at attention, he said, "Gentlemen, I am somewhat distressed by your apparent lack of respect for my orders."

Ashamed, the three RAF veterans bowed their heads. They had the highest respect for Colonel Harrison. Under no circumstances would they have disobeyed his orders without good reason.

"Colonel," Captain Dawson explained, "we did what we thought was in the best interest of the squadron and its men. We truly believed we had good cause for our actions, even if they violated orders or regulations."

Harrison looked at Captain Dawson and began to smile.

"I know that, Ted," he replied in a fatherly tone. "All three of you acted according to your training and experience. As a result, you saved lives. I'm recommending each of you for the Distinguished Flying Cross!"

The three men looked at each other, excited about their commendation, but more relieved that Colonel Harrison understood the reason for their actions. Then Harrison turned to the young boy standing beside Captain Dawson.

"As for you, Mr. Winslow," Colonel Harrison resumed his commanding tone. "I have also reviewed a report by Captain Simms which indicates you saved RAF pilots and property by delaying the flight of three Hurricanes. And through quick thinking, you helped our pilots scramble the remaining Spitfires to defend Hampton Airfield."

Colonel Harrison thoughtfully paused. He then continued, "This may be well and good, young man, however, I also have a directive here from RAF Fighter Command Headquarters. It demands strict adherence to policy regarding unauthorized personnel."

Harry's head dropped and his heart sank. Undoubtedly, Harry knew he was the "unauthorized personnel" the policy referred to. The thought of not being allowed on base caused Harry to feel weak in the knees.

Then Colonel Harrison sharply asked, "Captain Dawson, can you tell me the difference between authorized and unauthorized personnel?"

"Only those wearing Royal Air Force wings are authorized to be on an RAF base, sir!" Dawson snapped in reply.

Harry's stomach churned. Only the men and women of the Royal Air Force, those wearing the uniform RAF badge, were authorized to be on a military base. Twelve year old boys weren't allowed in the RAF. Fighting back tears, Harry wondered to himself if Captain Dawson would at least escort him off the base one last time.

Colonel Harrison stared at Harry. After a long pause he said, "Then, Mr. Winslow, I order you to wear this from now on!"

Confused, Harry looked at Harrison's outstretched hand. There, laying in the Colonel's palm was a brand new RAF wings badge. Not believing what was happening, Harry looked at Captain Dawson. When Dawson smiled and nodded at him, Harry reached to take the embroidered pin from Colonel Harrison. Speechless, Harry could hear his heart pounding in his chest.

Colonel Harrison continued, "All of you, listen. Contrary to what some people say, rules were not made to be broken! Rules were made for the safety and welfare of everyone. However, from time to time rules and orders might have to be reevaluated in light of particular circumstances. Thoughtful consideration of the rules and the manner with which they're applied is a sign of wisdom and the mark of leadership."

Sensitive to the lost look on Harry's face, Harrison reworded his point. "What I mean is, sometimes a situation occurs where one needs to break a rule in order to do what's best. But, you'd better be sure there's a good reason."

Colonel Harrison knew how important Harry was to the pilots of the 14th Squadron. Harry had proven himself a benefit to everyone at Hampton Airfield. As commander, it was Colonel Harrison's job to see that Fighter Command's orders were carried out. In this case, banishing Harry from the base would satisfy his orders, but all of Hampton Airfield would suffer for it.

A true leader, Colonel Harrison had wisely found a way to do what was best for everyone. By awarding Harry a set of wings, he changed the young boy's status from unauthorized to authorized. There might be someone in Fighter Command who would consider giving Harry RAF wings as disobeying orders. Even so, Colonel Harrison believed, without question, it was for good cause.

Captain Dawson bent down and softly spoke to Harry. "Colonel Harrison just made you my newest pilot officer. You're truly one of us, and we take care of our own. You're officially the thirteenth member of our squadron!"

Harry's sister, Susan, excitedly stepped through the door to help Harry fix the RAF wings to his worn blue-gray jacket. After giving him a hug and whispering in his 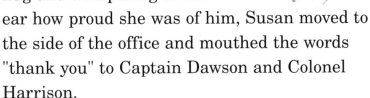 ear how proud she was of him, Susan moved to the side of the office and mouthed the words "thank you" to Captain Dawson and Colonel Harrison.

"Honorary Pilot Officer Winslow," Colonel Harrison started, "as long as you wear the RAF badge you are authorized to be on this base. However, as long as you are on this base you must obey orders and follow regulations. Do you understand?"

The 14th Squadron....stood at attention while their newest member walked past.

"Yes sir! I understand completely!" Harry replied.

"Very well then. Attention!" the Colonel shouted to everyone in the room. After the group snapped to attention Colonel Harrison finished, "You are all dismissed!"

Captains Dawson and Simms, Sergeant Pendleton, Harry and Susan stepped out of the office and into the corridor of the Operations Building. There, the rest of the pilots of the 14th Squadron lined the hallway. They respectfully stood at attention while their newest member walked past proudly wearing his RAF wings.

When Harry stepped out of the building to the field, everyone gathered around the young new pilot officer and cheered. Each one of them congratulated Harry on his honorary commission and a job well done.

CHAPTER FOURTEEN

THE MOST IMPORTANT REQUEST

After the commotion over Harry's promotion faded, Sergeant Pendleton stepped over and reached to shake hands with his young friend. Harry was a favorite with all the pilots and air crews, but Captain Dawson was closest to the boy. Dawson spent the most time with Harry, often with his mechanic, Sergeant Pendleton. It wasn't long before Harry had warmed a soft spot in the burly Sergeant's heart. Together, Dawson and Pendleton taught Harry everything they could about being a pilot and maintaining an airplane. The three of them formed a close friendship, regardless of their differences in age.

While the hands of the husky but soft-hearted sergeant and the twelve year old boy were shaking up and down, Harry began to apologize.

"I'm sorry I disobeyed your orders when I let the cat out of the bag."

Pendleton roared with laughter. Dropping

Harry's hand, he grabbed the boy by the shoulder and pulled him close.

"Don't worry about it, lad," the Sergeant began. "You were caught in a situation where you had to make a decision about what was best for everyone. Colonel Harrison knows what he's talking about. Wisdom is when experience, knowledge, and training all combine to tell you the right thing to do. And sometimes, it might mean disobeying orders. All I request is that you use your head when you make that decision. It's wrong to break rules for the sake of breaking rules. When you defy authority, you run the risk of disappointing the ones who mean the most to you. But if you can show there's a good reason, they'll understand. You did the right thing when it was needed."

Harry nodded at Pendleton's words. He was relieved the Sergeant understood why he let the cat out of the bag.

Thinking about Pendleton's request, Harry replied, "I'll follow the rules and make you proud of me, someday."

A soft smile brightened Sergeant Pendleton's face. Then he started to gently rub Harry's head of thick brown hair.

"You're wise beyond your years, Harry. We're proud of you already."

Across the airfield, most of the men had gathered around the fighter planes parked on the hardstand. Harry looked at his RAF wings and then at Sergeant Pendleton. Free to wander anywhere on the base, Harry tugged at Pendleton's arm. Together, the two members of the RAF walked off to join the other pilots and crew standing in front of the Spitfires.

An hour later, back in Colonel Harrison's office, Susan announced the arrival of a visitor, "Sir, there's a Mr. Tandy here to see you."

"Tandy?" Harrison asked. "Who is Mr. Tandy?"

Susan replied, "He says he's from Super-marine."

"Supermarine?" Harrison thought out loud. "What would he..."

Susan interrupted, "Perhaps you can ask him yourself, sir."

"Yes, of course," Harrison replied. "Send him in."

The man from Supermarine entered the room and greeted Colonel Harrison.

"Colonel, how do you do?" he started, and reached to shake Harrison's hand. "I'm Frederick Tandy from Supermarine."

Colonel Harrison looked at Mr. Tandy with some confusion. The past few days Harrison had been so busy supervising the repairs to the airfield, he had forgotten that Supermarine was sending an instructor to teach the pilots how to fly the new fighter planes.

"Sir," Tandy responded, "I have been sent here to train your pilots on flying the Spitfire."

"Oh, yes," Harrison recalled. A smile cracked Harrison's lips while he thought for a moment.

"Come here, Mr. Tandy," Colonel Harrison said while motioning for Tandy to follow him to the window. "Look out there."

Through the window, Harrison and Tandy could see almost the entire airfield. Out on the hardstand, stood the three Supermarine Spitfires. Next to the airplanes, the squadron members were gathered with Harry Winslow right in the middle of the group. There, in front of the other

pilots, Simms, Gainey, and Hyatt were using their hands to explain some of the Spitfire maneuvers they learned "the hard way". Harrison and Tandy watched the three pilots teach their lessons about the Spitfire. The rest of the men listen intently, completely absorbed in what was being said.

Harrison turned to the visitor. "You see, Tandy, you're a little late. I already have three experienced Spitfire instructors. Perhaps you could talk with them and pass on a few pointers. I must tell you, they seem to already have it jolly well down. You're welcome to stay here, but I know the lads in the 62nd Squadron really need you."

Surprised at the situation, Tandy replied, "Certainly, Colonel. I'll talk to your pilots. Maybe I can teach them a trick or two. After that I'll make an appointment with the the 62nd Squadron."

Mr. Tandy picked up his briefcase and left Colonel Harrison alone in his office. Laughing to himself, the Colonel returned to his desk and looked down at the stack of paperwork.

The very top requisition read, "Request for delivery of nine Supermarine Spitfire fighter planes with parts." In one quick sweeping movement of his hand, Harrison signed this most important requisition, and placed it in his "done" basket.

IN HINDSIGHT

On December 17, 1903, Orville and Wilbur Wright changed history. That morning, Orville flew the Wright Flyer, their fragile wood and fabric airplane, over the seaside beach at Kitty Hawk, North Carolina. Although it flew for only twelve seconds, the Wright Flyer had achieved the first powered flight of a heavier-than-air machine. Also on that historic day, Orville and Wilbur Wright made three more flights. The longest lasted fifty-seven seconds and covered a distance of 852 feet. Ever since, designers and engineers have tried to improve the capability and performance of aircraft to make them fly faster, farther and higher.

Soon, military commanders realized that enemy field positions could be readily observed from an airplane.

The Wright Flyer takes flight at Kitty Hawk.

In 1909, the Wright brothers supplied the United States Army with an improved version of the Wright Flyer to be used for reconnaissance. Many European countries like France, Germany and Britain developed their own airplanes for reconnaissance as well.

When World War I started in 1914, airplanes were immediately pressed into service by both sides in order to observe enemy positions. Ironically, no one considered what to do when two opposing enemy planes encountered each other. However, with the increasing number of airplanes being used to spy, eventually the issue would come to a head. At first, pilots carried hand guns and rifles in order to shoot at each other. As the war progressed, machine guns were fastened to the airplanes so that the pilot could better fly and shoot at the same time. From this humble beginning, the combat fighter plane was born.

Although still made of wood, wire and fabric, the biplanes (two wings) and triplanes (three wings) of World War I were remarkable improvements over the airplanes built just ten years earlier. Using the most powerful engines available (150-200 horsepower), the new fighter planes could carry machine guns as well as a few small bombs. Although primitive by todays standards, these planes represented leading edge technology at the time and they changed the face of the war forever.

World War I German "Albatross".

After World War I, the excitement of international airplane racing contests fueled the need for further advancement in aircraft. As bigger engines resulted in increased speed, so did the need for greater aerodynamic design and stronger materials. Wood and fabric bodies with wings held by wires couldn't withstand the force and stress encountered when engines producing over 1000 horsepower hurled planes faster than 300 miles per hour. Sadly, many racing pilots crashed when the wings or tails tore off their airplanes at high speeds. High speed flight required streamline single wing planes built with metal frames, fitted with metal skin. As racing demanded pilots to fly faster, the newer single wing metal planes became standard. By the end of 1935, even the most advanced wood and fabric biplanes had become obsolete.

At the onset of World War II, the German Luftwaffe was by far the most superior air force in the world. German technical improvements in aircraft design, much of it learned from airplane racing competition, resulted in the development of single wing fighter planes

that could reach speeds greater than 350 miles per hour.
When the Luftwaffe lead the German forces into Poland in
1939, the older biplanes flown by the Polish Air Force
were no match for the speed and power of the new sleek
German fighter planes. In time, the French and Belgium
Air Forces, also flying outdated aircraft, would learn the
same costly lesson.

Wary of the remarkable aircraft advancements
being made by the Germans throughout the 1930s, British
airplane designers continued their research and tested new
aircraft designs. In 1935, the British manufacturer
Hawker developed a rugged single wing fighter utilizing
the 1030 horsepower Merlin engine that could fly faster
than 300 miles per hour. To make it more resistant to the
stress of this speed, metal skin was used on the wings and
front of the plane. A left over from the previous genera-
tion of aircraft, the back of the fuselage however, still
utilized fabric stretched over an aluminum frame. The
fighter was called the Hawker "Hurricane".

Another British aircraft company, Supermarine,
developed what would become known as one of the finest
fighter planes ever designed. In 1936, the first
Supermarine "Spitfire" prototype was flown by the RAF.
The Spitfire utilized a radical elliptical wing design and a
more powerful engine to give it superior flight performance.

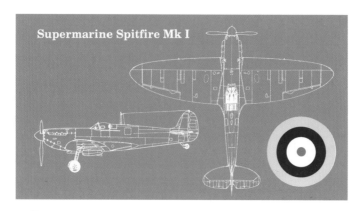

Supermarine Spitfire Mk I

By the spring of 1940, England raced to fill squadrons with new Spitfires and Hawker Hurricanes in preparation of war. Only by the thinnest of margins were enough Hurricanes and Spitfires produced for the pilots of the RAF to save England from defeat at the hands of the Luftwaffe in the Battle of Britain.

Although designers hurried to create faster more powerful fighters during the war, it took years to design and produce new types of planes. As a result, the existing designs were constantly updated and improved to provide even the slightest edge over the enemy. Larger engines, and modifications in wing design were often quickly made to increase the speed and effectiveness of existing aircraft on both sides.

Unfortunately, limitations in the basic design of aircraft are encountered at some point. The Hawker Hurricane, eventually could not be improved upon any further and was all but retired by the end of 1943. However, the more advanced aerodynamic design of the Supermarine Spitfire allowed it to continue in service throughout the duration of the war. By 1945, the Spitfire design had been modified over twenty times to improve the original fighter plane.

However, by the end of the war, a revolution in aircraft design occurred. Development of the jet engine promised to propel fighter planes faster than any piston engine could. The age of the jet fighter plane was born. After 1945, the piston engine, propeller driven airplane would begin to fade from the rolls of combat fighters. Jet fighters could fly faster, farther and higher than anything ever created before.

GLOSSARY

Armistice: A cease fire or end of a war. Veterans Day celebrates the Armistice declared to end World War I on November 11, 1918.

Blast Pen: A parking area for aircraft surrounded by an earthen fence used to shield the plane from damage caused by an explosion.

Captain: A military officer ranking below colonel and above lieutenant.

Distinguished Flying Cross: A medal awarded for heroism.

Fuselage: The central body of an airplane.

Hardstand: A hard surfaced area next to an airstrip used for parking planes and ground vehicles.

Hawker Hurricane: A type of British plane.

Hedgerow: A row of bushes or small trees that form a fence.

Intercept: To stop or interrupt the progress of enemy aircraft.

Junkers Ju 87: A German two-seat dive bomber (also Stuka).

Lieutenant: A military officer ranking below captain.

Lorry: An English term for a truck or transport vehicle.

Messerschmitt 109: A type of German fighter plane (also Me 109).

Operations Building: The airfield's central administration building.

RAF Wings: The badge worn by members of the Royal Air Force.

Requisition: Paperwork or forms used to order supplies.

Row: An English term for fight.

Scramble: The immediate launch of airplanes from the airfield.

Stick or Yoke: The control stick of an airplane used for steering.

Stockade: Military term for jail or prison.

Supermarine Spitfire: A type of British fighter plane (also Spit).